delivered by

HOW TO BUILD OUR WORLD

Raise a
RAINFOREST

By William Anthony

BookLife PUBLISHING

©2021
BookLife Publishing Ltd.
King's Lynn
Norfolk PE30 4LS

A catalogue record for this book is available from the British Library.

ISBN: 978-1-83927-261-5

Written by:
William Anthony

Edited by:
John Wood

Designed by:
Jasmine Pointer

All facts, statistics, web addresses and URLs in this book were verified as valid and accurate at time of writing. No responsibility for any changes to external websites or references can be accepted by either the author or publisher.

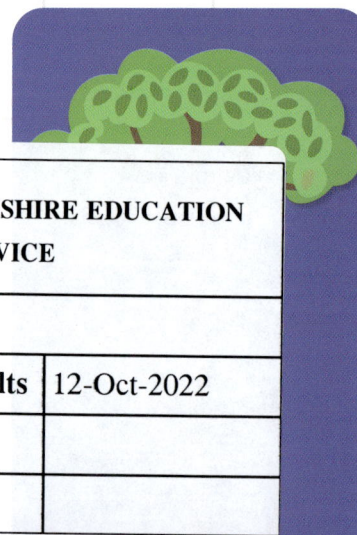

Image Credits

All images are courtesy of Shutterstock.com, unless otherwise specified. With thanks to Getty Images, Thinkstock Photo and iStockphoto.

Cover – Svvell Design, derter, IconBunny, Alexandr Vorobev, Sorn340 Studio Images, David Jara Bogunya. 4–5 – Ardea-studio, avian, Kirasolly, Alex Oakenman, MaryDesy, worldclassphoto, BorneoRimbawan. 6–7 – Elena Paletskaya, Ksusha Dusmikeeva, GoodStudio, Jakob Weyde, Avigator Fortuner, szefei. 8–9 – Kirasolly, leungchopan, KarenHBlack, raditya. 10–11 – AustralianCamera, Sara Berdon, Chansom Pantip. 12–13 – BorneoRimbawan. 14–15 – POKPAK101, Kathryn L. Schipper, Uwe Bergwitz. 16–17 – Koshevnyk, barkarola, Andrew Krasovitckii, Vladimir Wrangel, outdoorsman, Kamran Karimov, funnybear36, Bildagentur Zoonar GmbH. 18–19 – NotionPic, Andrew Krasovitckii, Ondrej Prosicky, Ken Griffiths, Pesek Photo, Evgeniya Mokeeva, H.Elvin, Vectors Bang. 20–21 – olesia_g, Rich Carey, VikiVector, Halfpoint, Syda Productions, HappyPictures, Enric Adell Illustration. 22–23 – olnik_y, Virinaflora, SunshineVector.

Contents

Words that look like **this** can be found in the glossary on page 24.

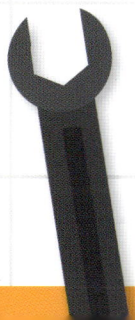

How to Build Our World

Our world is amazing. It is full of different places to go and wonderful things to see.

Earth is made up of many different **environments**, from rainforests to cities.

Each environment is home to different animals and people. There are different plants, buildings and objects too. No two environments are the same.

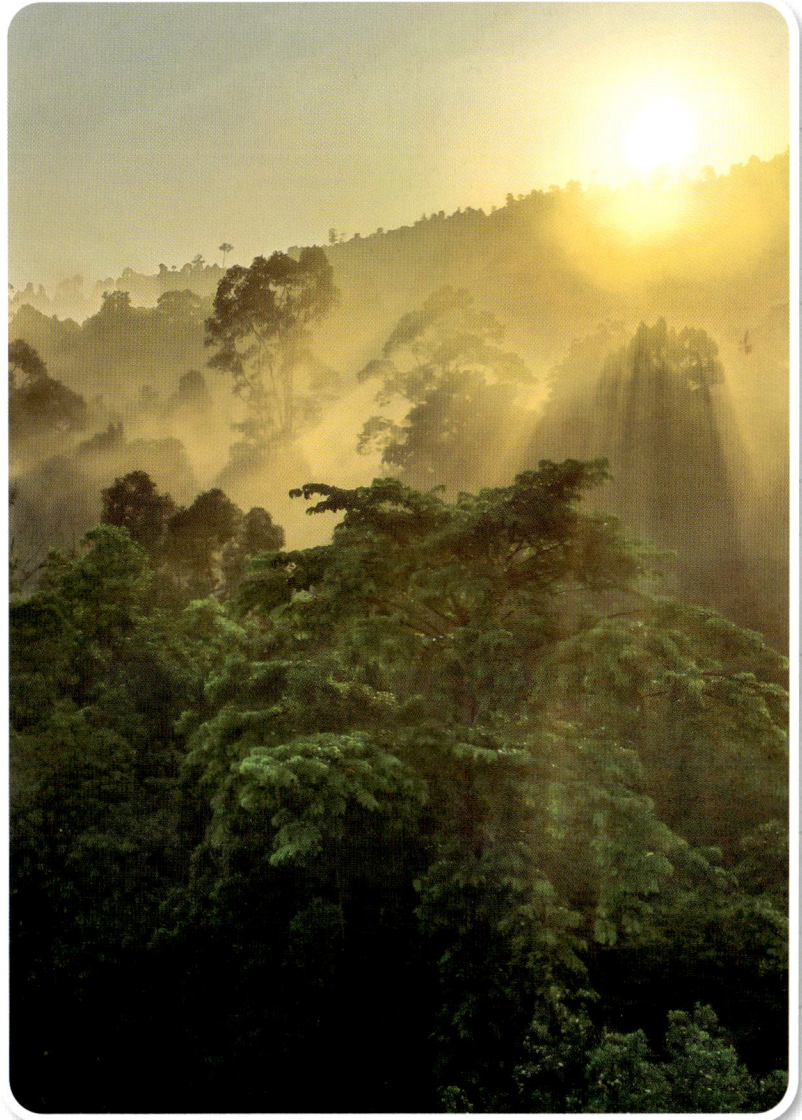

But what makes up each environment? Let's take a look at how we would build a rainforest environment from scratch...

Step One:
Fit the Forest Floor

Rainforests have lots of different layers. The lowest layer is the forest floor. Lots of things will live down there. Let's get started.

Bugs and **fungi** live on the forest floor. They break down dead plants and animals.

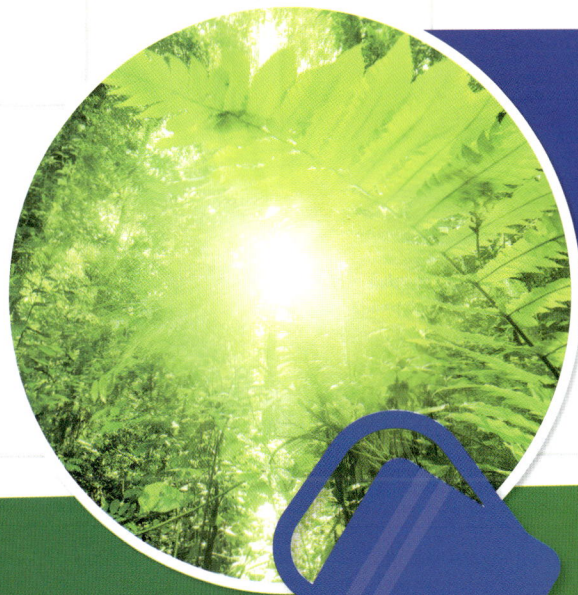

When the other layers are built, only a tiny bit of sunlight will reach the forest floor.

When we add the animals later, some of them will live in or beside this river. It will also give them a place to drink water.

7

Unveil the Understorey

Let's start building upwards! The next layer we need to add is the understorey layer.

Rainforests aren't just made up of giant trees. In the understorey layer, there are small trees and tall **shrubs**.

Many of the shrubs in the understorey layer grow bright, colourful flowers.

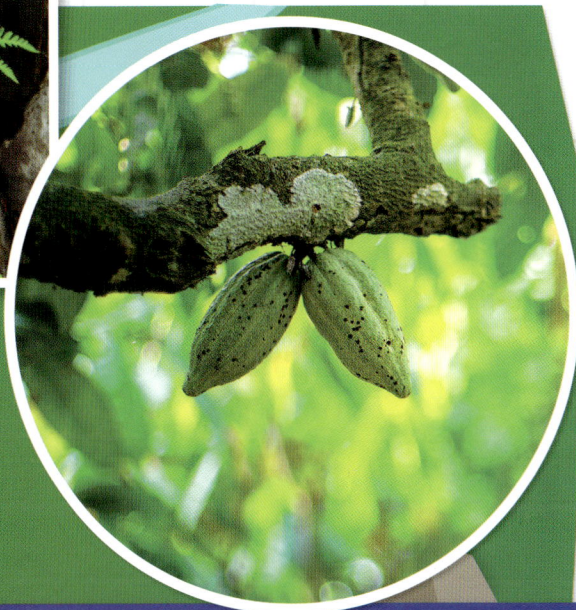

Other shrubs grow fruits. This is important for the animals that we will add later. They will have fruit to eat.

Step Three:
Construct the Canopy

The layer of treetops above the understorey layer is called the canopy. Let's add it in!

Can you see how many treetops are in the canopy? There are lots! The canopy acts like a big, leafy roof for the rainforest.

The canopy blocks out lots of sunshine. This is why the forest floor does not have much light.

The canopy is full of fruits and nuts that grow on trees all year round. There will be lots of food for the animals!

Add the Emergent Layer

The last layer we need to add to our rainforest is the emergent layer. Let's set it up!

The tallest trees in the rainforest are part of the emergent layer. These trees can be up to 70 metres tall.

The emergent layer usually gets lots of bright sunlight.

Because the emergent layer is so open above the canopy, it can be very windy. In fact, let's set up the weather...

Set up the Weather

An important part of raising a rainforest is adding the weather. Weather is what you can see in the sky and feel in the air outside.

Rainforests are called rainforests because they get lots of rain! Over two metres of rain can fall in just one year.

Because many rainforests are near the **Equator**, the **temperature** stays the same during most of the year — warm!

The top layers are packed with plants. That means one raindrop can take ten minutes to get from the emergent layer to the forest floor!

Add the Animals

It's time to add animals to our rainforest. Even though rainforests only cover a small part of our planet, over one-half of the planet's animal and plant **species** live there.

Some rainforests have rivers. Animals that live in rainforest rivers around the world include crocodiles, dolphins and many more.

The forest floor is home to many minibeasts, such as ants and worms.

Many animals live in the small understorey trees. Some snakes can climb into trees, even though they have no arms or legs!

Farther up the trees, the animals are very different to the ones near the ground. Let's add some animals to the canopy and emergent layers.

The emergent layer is home to lots of birds. The scarlet macaw lives among the tallest trees.

The branches and leaves in the tallest trees can be **unstable**. Lots of animals, such as the pygmy glider, move between trees by **gliding** or flying.

Animals that cannot fly or glide need to be able to move quickly and easily. Capuchin monkeys are one of these animals.

Protect the Place

Rainforests are not just wonderful and beautiful – they are very important for our planet. However, humans are causing lots of harm to rainforests.

Lots of trees are being cut down. This is called deforestation. This is bad because trees clean the air for us by taking in **carbon dioxide**.

We can help to protect rainforest environments. Many **charities** do lots of work to stop deforestation.

Some charities plant trees when others are cut down. This stops rainforests disappearing completely.

Design Your Own Environment

Our new rainforest looks incredible! It has everything from awesome animals to the tallest trees. It's time to design your own environment. Grab a pencil, a rubber and some paper...

What will your environment's floor be made from — sand, grass or something else?

Will your environment have plants, such as trees?

Which animals will live in your environment?

23

Glossary

carbon dioxide	a thing that is found in the air that humans breathe out
charities	groups that try to help people, animals or other things
environments	the different parts of our world that people, animals and plants live in
Equator	the imaginary line around the Earth that is an equal distance from the North and South Poles
fungi	living things that look like plants but have no flowers
gliding	to fly or move smoothly through the air without effort
shrubs	a type of small plant
species	a group of very similar animals or plants that can create young together
temperature	how hot or cold something is
unstable	likely to move around or fall

Index